This book belongs to:

Barnabas Bluebird

and the
BB3

Story and Photography by

Margie K. Carroll

Margie Carroll Press
Holly Springs, Georgia

Special thanks to Gloria, Doris, Carol, and Linda.

Margie Carroll Press
P.O. Box 581
Holly Springs, GA 30142

For my Bird Watcher Friends

Hello, Friend!
My name is Barnabas.

Today my three sisters and
I fledged our nest.
We fluttered onto a limb
and stared in amazement.

"So bright! So breezy! So beautiful!" we gasped.
Mom and Dad proudly watched from the treetop.
Dad announced our names to the neighborhood.

Wait just a minute!
We must not begin this way.
Let's go back to the beginning of my story.

Meet Dad and Mom.
According to them, this is our family's story.

Dad spied Mom one early morning in spring.

Her soft feathers, fluffed against the chilly fog, attracted him.

He waved.

"Hmmm, very handsome," thought Mom.

They became inseparable and began house-hunting.

"This one is nice and shady," Dad remarked.

"No, too rustic."

"What about this one, Dear?"
Dad suggested.

"Hmmm."

"Heavens no! The entrance is irregular," rejected Mom.

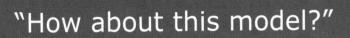
"How about this model?"

"No, too breezy!"

"This one is perfect!"

"Perfect indeed! We shall build our nest here!"

Mom brought pine needles for the nest.

Dad helped too.

Building the nest took lots of time and effort.

Dad added one more pine needle to the nest.

He was surprised to see four perfect eggs!

Mom sat on the eggs for two long weeks.

One morning Dad brought
Mom some breakfast.

"What a wonderful surprise!"
exclaimed Dad.

I hatched first. They named me Barnabas after my dad.
My three sisters were temporarily named BB1, BB2, and BB3.

"Mom, Barnabas is named after Dad. Why don't we have real names?" asked the girls.

"Darlings, I was given an unfortunate name for a bluebird. Therefore, I am going to let you name yourselves when you fledge the nest. The first thing you see that starts with the letter 'B' will be your name," she explained.

"What is your name, Mom?" I asked.

"Robin."

Mostly we ate and slept. Mom and Dad brought us tasty treats.

They peeked in the nest and watched us sleep.

At first our nest was roomy, but we grew quickly!

We ate

worms,

moths,

caterpillars,

spiders,

crickets,

grasshoppers,

beetles,

ants,

katydids,

and berries!

Before long the nest became crowded and tempers flared.
The girls seemed so innocent, but they could be irritating!
Sometimes I had to complain to Dad and Mom.

"BB1 gets all the good bugs!
BB2 is hopping around and I can't sleep!
And, they are teasing BB3!" I reported to Dad.

"Barnabas, the girls are asleep. Stop tattling, Son."

BB1, "Burrrrrrrrp!"

BB2, "Tee hee, tee hee!"

BB3, "Thanks, Barnabas.

"I wish I had brothers!"
I complained.

From inside our nest, we peeked at the neighborhood.

BB1 saw a butterfly.
"Oh, I hope I first see a butterfly when I fledge! Then my name will be BB Butterfly."

BB2 saw a bumblebee and declared that "BB Bumblebee" would be a perfect name for her.

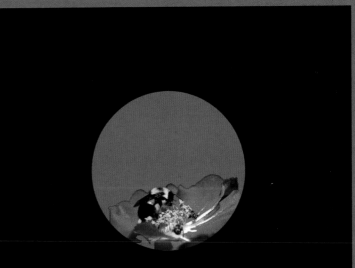

Poor BB3 did not know what to wish for because she didn't know what a "B" was.
She asked me to help her with this dilemma.

"Okay, I'll be thinking," I replied.

We watched our neighbors and asked lots of questions.

"Oh, that is a Tufted Titmouse. He eats seeds and is frisky," offered Mom.

"That is a chickadee."

"That is a wren."

We were homeschooled.

"That is a cardinal."

"That is a squirrel."

"YIKES!" we gasped.

"That's just nosy Mr. Cardinal," Mom said.
"He is curious looking, but quite harmless."

Soon we were ready to leave the nest. Dad and Mom brought many insects to give me strength for my first flight. I fluttered to a nearby limb.

Dad brought me a huge caterpillar.

"Barnabas, tell us the first thing the girls see that starts with the letter 'B.'"

"Okay!" I replied excitedly.

BB1 leaned down and gobbled a cricket. Finally, she fledged and looked up.

"She saw a **buzzard**!" I exclaimed.

Mom gasped, "A **buzzard**?"

"Well, that's nice, Darling.
They can eat almost anything."

BB2 emerged next from the nest. She hopped along the limb and looked down.

"Mom, Dad!
BB2 saw a **bullfrog**!" I reported.

"A **bullfrog**? Well they . . .
they hop well and are moist,"
Dad stumbled.

"I did NOT see a bullfrog, and
BB1 did NOT see a buzzard!
I saw a bumblebee, and she
saw a butterfly," declared BB2.

"Now, Barnabas, think hard. What did the girls really see when they fledged?" Mom asked.

"Now I remember. They saw a butterfly and a bumblebee."

I waited for BB3 to fledge.

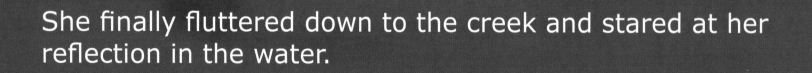

She finally fluttered down to the creek and stared at her reflection in the water.

"Mom! Dad! BB3 saw **BEAUTY!**" I yelled.

"Oh, how delightful!" they exclaimed.

Dad flew to the treetops and signaled with his wings.

"Mrs. Bluebird and I are proud to introduce our new fledglings to the neighborhood. Please welcome Barnabas, BB Butterfly, BB Bumblebee, and BB Beauty."

This has been our story my friend. You are welcome to visit our neighborhood any time!

Your friend,

Barnabas

Bluebird Bits

Eastern Bluebirds live in open country around trees, but with little understory and sparse ground cover.

Eastern Bluebirds eat mostly insects, wild fruit, and berries. Insects caught on the ground are a bluebird's main food. Major prey include caterpillars, beetles, crickets, grasshoppers, and spiders. In fall and winter, bluebirds eat large amounts of fruit including currants, mistletoe, sumac, blueberries, black cherry, wild holly, dogwood berries, honeysuckle, and juniper berries. Rarely, Eastern Bluebirds have been recorded eating snakes, lizards, and tree frogs.

A male Eastern Bluebird attracts a female to his nest site by carrying material in and out of the hole, perching, and fluttering his wings. The female does the nest building. She makes the nest by loosely weaving together grasses and pine needles, then lining it with fine grasses. Bluebirds may use the same nest for multiple broods. Eastern Bluebirds typically have more than one successful brood per year. Young produced in early nests usually leave their parents in summer, but young from later nests frequently stay with their parents over the winter.

Clutch Size: 2–7 eggs
Incubation Period: 11–19 days
Nestling Period: 17–21 days
Egg Description: Pale blue or, rarely, white.
Condition at Hatching: Naked except for sparse tufts of gray down, eyes closed.

Bluebird populations fell in the early twentieth century. But in the 1960s and 1970s establishment of bluebird trails and other nest box campaigns helped Eastern Bluebird numbers to recover.

Resource Vocabulary

- brood: a number of young produced or hatched at one time; a family of offspring or young

- cavities: any hollow place; hollow

- clutch: a hatch of eggs; the number of eggs produced or incubated at one time

- display: pattern of behavior in birds, fishes, etc. by which the animal attracts attention while it is courting the female

- environment: the external surroundings in which a plant or animal lives, which tend to influence its development and behavior

- fledge: to feed and care for (a young bird) until it is able to fly

- fledgling: a young bird that has just grown the feathers needed to fly and is capable of surviving outside the nest

- forage: the act of searching for food or provisions

- habitat: the natural environment of an organism; place that is natural for the life and growth of an organism

- hatch: to bring forth (young) from the egg

- incubate: to supply (eggs) with heat for their development, by sitting on them

- pair bond: the temporary or permanent association formed between a female and male animal during courtship and mating

- perch: a pole, branch, or other resting place above ground on which a bird roosts or alights

- prey: an animal hunted or captured by another for food

- territory: a geographic area occupied by a single animal, mating pair, or group

Questions for Young Readers

Barnabas hatched before his sisters. T or F   true

How many eggs were in the nest?   four

What color were the eggs?   light blue

How many brothers did Barnabas have?   none

Were his mom and dad good providers?   yes

Could Barnabas and his sisters see out of their nest?   yes

What were pine needles used for in the story?   nesting material

Why did Barnabas complain about his sisters?   BB1 ate too much, BB2 hopped too much, and they teased BB3.

Did his dad believe him?   No, he thought they were sleeping.

Did BB1 and BB2 really see a buzzard and a bullfrog?   Well, that's for you to decide!

Margie K. Carroll is a retired educator, Media Specialist, computer programmer, and Technology Specialist. She enjoys writing, bicycling, traveling, and wildlife photography.

Observing and photographing animal behavior is a fascinating second career. Margie's book series for children uses her photography and storytelling skills to illuminate an animal family's experiences from the point of view of their offspring.

Margie lives in Canton, Georgia, where she enjoys the company of deer, raccoons, rabbits, numerous song birds, and several alert cats at her studio in the woods.

I make designs using my animal photography. These "Animasques" can be tricky.
Can you spot the bluebirds?

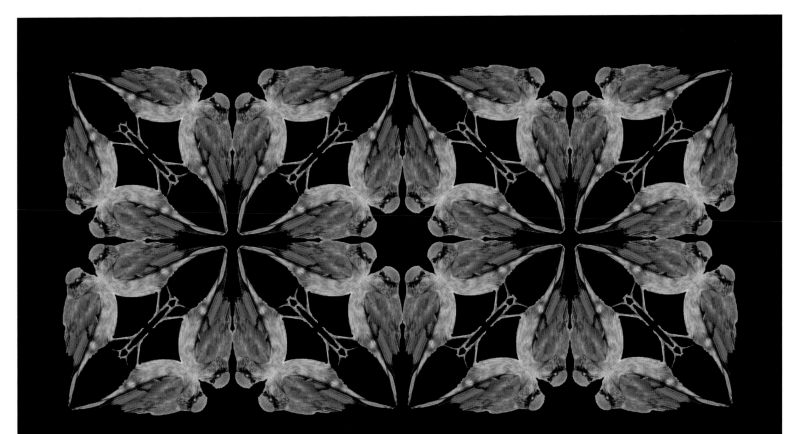

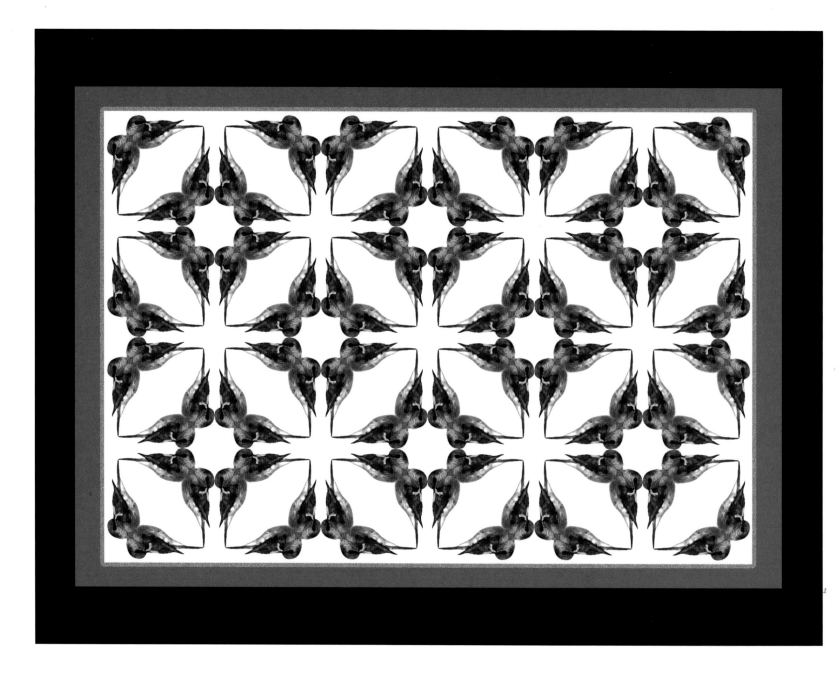

Be creative and cherish wildlife!